Anonymous

Tourists' guide for pleasure trips to the summer resorts, sea bathing and watering places

Anonymous

Tourists' guide for pleasure trips to the summer resorts, sea bathing and watering places

ISBN/EAN: 9783337147211

Printed in Europe, USA, Canada, Australia, Japan

Cover: Foto ©Andreas Hilbeck / pixelio.de

More available books at **www.hansebooks.com**

PRICE 25 CENTS TOURISTS' GUIDE

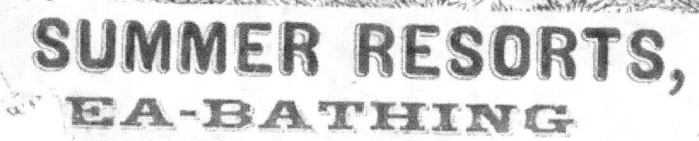

SUMMER RESORTS,
SEA-BATHING
AND
WATERING PLACES.

SUMMER SCHEDULES 1878.

THIS TIME TABLE has been carefully prepared and is respectfully presented for the use of Guests at the Springs, and other Summer Resorts, who contemplate visiting Baltimore.

B. & O. R. R.

Leave Grafton,	9.15 P.M.	10.18 P.M. 10.20 A.M.
" Oakland,	10.11 "	12.17 A.M. 12.21 P.M.
" Deer Park,	10.25 "	12.30 " 12.35 "
" Cumberland	12.20 A.M.	2.30 " 2.50 "
" Sir John's R.	1.49 "	4.00 " 4.23 "
" Harper's F'y	3.17 "	5.31 " 5.59 "
" Washington	5.15 "	7.40 " 8.10 "
Arr at Baltimore	6.20 "	8.40 " 9.10 "

VALLEY BRANCH

Leave Staunton	6.15 A.M.	11.15 A.M.
" Weyer's Cave Station	6.57 "	11.47 "
" Harrisonburg	7.45 "	12.15 P.M.
" Mount Jackson	10.25 "	1.29 "
" Capon Springs Road	1.05 P.M.	3.17 "
" Winchester	3.00 "	4.11 "
" Harper's Ferry	5.56 "	5.35 "

Thence by B. & O., as above, to Baltimore.

N. C. & PENN'A R. R.

" 'ius Glen	8.00 A.M.	8.35 P.M.
" Fa...	9.05 "	9.30 "
" ...nsport	12.40 P.M.	12.35 A.M.
" ...	4.25 "	6.40 A.M. 4.20 "
" ...	5.27 "	7.55 " 5.24 "
" ...	7.30 "	10.35 " 7.25 "

W. C. V. M. & G. S. R. R.

Leave Danville	9.25 A.M. 10.10 P.M
" Lynchburgh	1.30 P.M. 11.23 A.M.
" Charlottesville	4.00 " 2.45 "
" Gordonsville	4.52 " 3.35 "
" Alexandria	8.50 " 7.35 "
" Washington	9.15 " 8.00 "
" Baltimore, via B. & P.	11.10 " 10.10 "
do. via B. & O.	10.35 " 9.30 "

C. & O. R. R.

Leave Huntington	10.00 A.M. 6.30 P.M.
" Wh. Sulphur Springs	7.30 P.M. 8.45 A.M.
" Alleghany Station	7.46 " 9.01 "
" Covington	9.00 " 9.50 "
" Goshen	10.47 " 11.59 "
" Staunton	12.25 A.M. 1.35 P.M.
" Charlottesville	2.30 " 3.50 "
" Gordonsville	3.30 " 4.45 "

Thence by Va. Midland R.R. as above to Baltimore, or from Staunton by Valley Branch and B. & O.

A. M. & O. R. R.

Leave Bristol	4.30 A.M. 11.25 P.M.
" Christiansburg	9.32 " 4.41 A.M.
" Big Tunnel	9.47 " 4.58 "
" Alleghany	9.57 " 5.09 "
" Salem	10.36 " 5.51 "
" Blue Ridge Springs	11.22 " 6.40 "
" Lynchburg	1.00 P.M. 8.45 A.M.

Thence by Va. Midland as above to Baltimore or by A. M. & O. R. R. to Burkeville, and via Richmond to Baltimore, or via Norfolk and by Bay Line Steamers leaving Norfolk daily 6 P. M. and Old Point at 7 P. M.

FALLING SPRING FALLS, VA.

FOR

Pleasure Trips

TO THE

Summer Resorts,

SEA BATHING

AND

WATERING PLACES

CONVENIENT TO

AND ITS VICINITY

Price, Twenty-Five Cents.

HAGADORN BROTHERS, 5 S. CALVERT ST. BALTIMORE.

Entered according to the Act of Congress, in the year 1878,
by Francis L. Hagadorn, in the Office of the Librarian of Congress.

PUBLISHER'S PREFACE.

The chief difficulty in the way of the auspicious introduction of a work like this, is to awaken the active interest of those whom it is the object of the Publishers primarily to serve. To present to those in quest of health or pleasure a comprehensive survey of the various routes opening up in every direction from Baltimore, it is necessary to enlist the co-operation not only of those controlling rival routes of travel, but rival hostelries, sea-side resorts, mineral regions and mountain retreats of every description.

The great variety of these, accessible to Baltimore, adds not only to the attractive field which we have chosen for our work, but multiplies by its very attractiveness the difficulties of the undertaking.

Whatever discrepancies or short-comings may be detected in this First Edition, must therefore be attributed to these natural obstacles, which by presenting themselves, have not only sharpened our appetite for ultimate success, but have indicated to us the lines that lead to it.

No effort will be spared, on the part of the publishers, to make the succeeding editions of their "Guide" more and more worthy of patronage and confidence; as from the very nature of the work, it cannot be made subservient to any peculiar interests, but those of the TOURIST, seeking from this centre the various Routes of Travel that open up to him the fields of pleasure, or sources of healthful recreation, so bountifully bestowed throughout this favored region. Leaving the analysis of waters, or the details of rail-road, or steamboat or hotel accommodations to those who choose to avail themselves of our advertising pages, we aim to show the general scope of those attractive fields lying at our very doors, and invite the attention of the Tourist to the fact that within a few hour's travel in almost every direction, we have not only the Surf of the Ocean, but Hot Springs, Glaciers,* Caves, Grottoes Lakes, Mountains, and pastoral attractions which rival many of those allurements of travel so attractively set forth in European Guide Books.

---

* The Ice Mountain of Virginia.

TOURISTS' GUIDE.

NEARLY two hundred and fifty years ago, LEONARD CALVERT planted on the shores of the Chesapeake Bay, the seeds of the noble little Commonwealth that bears the name of his adored Queen MARY, (*Mary* land) whose metropolis perpetuates his lordly title—

"BALTIMORE."

BALTIMORE CITY HALL.

The city was incorporated 1745: in 1752 it began to show signs of life, had a fleet of two vessels,—the fore-runners of the famous "Baltimore Clippers," which subsequently became a terror to British commerce.

Its location, seemingly accidental, must have been determined by a more prophetic wisdom than man's. It combines more advantages than any other on the Atlantic coast, being both a seaport and an inland city, with a spacious, deep, protected harbor, and is at the same time nearer to all the trading centres and granaries of the West and Northwest.

ITS IMMEDIATE SURROUNDINGS are beautiful. Situated on a succession of hills, above smiling valleys through which sparkling streams glide to the Bay, she sits like a queen, with her monuments and spires piercing the air.

BATTLE MONUMENT.

WILDEY MONUMENT.

BALTIMORE has many attractions for travelers, especially in the early summer and autumn, when its surrounding scenery is newly dressed with living green, or tinged with a gorgeous array of colors.

The places of interest which the tourist will visit while in the city, are Peabody Institute, containing 65,000 volumes and a number of pieces of statuary, chief of which is Rinehart's exquisite chef-de-œuvre, "Clytie;" the Academy of Music; Johns Hopkins University;

GREENMOUNT.

ENTRANCE TO DRUID HILL.

Greenmount Cemetery; Druid Hill Park, whose natural

grandeur is said to excel that of any park in the world; and Eutaw Place, which has recently been elegantly improved with parks, shrubbery and fountains.

In order to give the reader a bird's-eye view, let us ascend

WASHINGTON MONUMENT,

a graceful Doric column of white marble, surmounted by a gigantic statue of George Washington. On the balcony we stand 280 feet above the Bay.

WASHINGTON MONUMENT.

The place which surrounds it is called Mt. Vernon Place, where are the mansions of the wealthy and elite. Below us is the Peabody Institute, Mt. Vernon M. E.

PEABODY INSTITUTE.

MT. VERNON CHURCH.

Church, and, three squares away, the elegant spire of the

First Presbyterian Church. To the north, Charles street avenue stretches away, opening a beautiful vista. To the east the city crowds together in the valley and spreads over the hills, crowned in the distance by Patterson Park. To the west and northwest there is a continuous ascent, terminating at the surrounding woods and

DRUID HILL PARK.

EDMUND'S WELL.

LAKE SCENE IN PARK.

Here there are beautiful drives in every direction, through wild-wood glens, over hills and valleys, cultivated and adorned with high art.

North of the Park, reposing in the valley of Jones' Falls, is the village of Woodberry, the Lowell of Maryland. On every side extends a living panorama, unexcelled for simple beauty.

Turning to the south the eye rests upon a wide expanse of water, sparkling in the sun like an immense mirror: it is

CHESAPEAKE BAY.

a magnificent sheet of water, which no traveler should fail to traverse. It is closely identified with the civil and commercial history of our country.

This view of Baltimore, with its myriad houses, its monuments, its temples, its avenues, bay and rivers, its parks and surrounding scenery, is truly grand and is literally unsurpassed.

THE OLD BAY LINE ROUTE,
To Old Point Comfort, Norfolk, Portsmouth, and the South.

From Baltimore we propose taking the tourist along the various routes of travel to the principal places of interest which have connections with it by rail or water.

Let our first trip be on

THE CHESAPEAKE BAY,

taking the "OLD BAY LINE" steamers which for more than a half century have been running this route, signally exempt from casualties. We first steam by Locust Point and Canton, the tidewater termini of the Baltimore and Ohio and Northern Central Railways. At the extreme end, below Locust Point, is

FORT M'HENRY,

with the stars and stripes waving over its ramparts. It was during its bombardment in 1814 that Francis S. Key, a Baltimorean and prisoner on one of the British ships, seeing "'mid the rocket's red glare" the flag of his country "still waving in air," composed the immortal song, "THE STAR-SPANGLED BANNER."

Seven miles below is FORT CARROLL, a large stone fort, in an unfinished state, standing in the midst of the waters, to protect the channel and entrance to the harbor.

HOLLY GROVE, on the northern shore of the Patapsco River, is a noted place for summer recreation, to which boats make several trips a day during the season.

NORTH POINT, next below, known by the two light-houses, is where the British engaged the Americans in the battle of North Point, September 12, 1814. This

THE BAY LINE

FOR NORFOLK,
PORTSMOUTH,
THE SOUTH and SOUTH-WEST.

THE BAY LINE
Comprises the new and elegant Steamers

CAROLINA and FLORIDA,

Leaving Union Dock, Baltimore, 6 p. m.
(Canton Wharf, foot of Chesapeake st., at 7.30 p. m.)
ON ARRIVAL OF NORTHERN & EASTERN TRAINS,
Touching at Old Point Comfort, where is located

THE SPLENDID HYGEIA HOTEL,
A delightful resort at all seasons of the year.

All the comforts of a First-Class Hotel are afforded on these Steamers, superior State-Room accommodations, and the Tables acknowledged to be unsurpassed in every respect. Fruits, Fish, Game, &c, in season.

Canton Cars of Madison Avenue Line, run every fifteen minutes to corner of Elliott and Chesapeake streets, one square from steamer. For tickets and information apply at Company's office, 157 West Baltimore st. Baltimore.

E. BROWN, G. T. A.   WM. M. LAWSON, Agent.

engagement saved Baltimore from capture: so well appreciated by the citizens, that in 1815 they erected the BATTLE MONUMENT to commemorate its heroes. This stands in Monument Square, an unique and handsome shaft, which gave to the city its soubriquet "The Monumental City."

Passing the SEVEN-FOOT KNOLL LIGHT-HOUSE, an iron structure standing out of the waters, we enter the *Bay*. The waters expand into the proportions of a sea; and the distant banks, with their green rolling hills and shifting scenery, add fresh pleasure to the sail.

Forty miles below Baltimore, in the distance, we discern the quaint old capital of Maryland—ANNAPOLIS, the dome of the State House being distinctly visible. The approach by water gives a fine view of this old city, the elegant grounds of the Naval School and the surrounding shores. We reach Annapolis either by rail or regular steam packet from Baltimore.

On the opposite side of the Bay is the EASTERN SHORE, justly considered by its worthy inhabitants the paradise of the Western World. The customs of old English society were, until quite recently, preserved among them, and they still spend much of their time in fishing, hunting, racing, &c. But the old times are passing away, and the towns are becoming modernized. The principal ones are Oxford, Easton, and Cambridge.

FAIR HAVEN, on the Western shore, 80 miles below Baltimore, is a quiet lovely resort, where every accommodation for health and pleasure is provided.

We pass the night on the widest parts of the Bay, gently lulled to sleep by the slow and even rollings of the Horse-Shoe bend, and in the grey of the morning are awakened by the steam whistle at Old Point Comfort.

THE HYGEIA HOTEL, OLD POINT COMFORT, Va.

Situated within one hundred yards of Fortress Monroe. Open all the year, with ample capacity for 400 guests. Has all modern improvements, elevator, gas and electric bells in every room; water, bath-rooms and closets on each floor. Six daily Mails and Telegraph Office. Fifteen to twenty first-class Steamers land daily except Sunday, 150 yards from the door. Rooms and halls comfortably heated, and every comfort provided for tourists and health seekers during the winter. Fire-Escapes only fifty feet apart on every floor. Superior beach for bathing at door-steps, and good from May until November.— Boating, fishing and driving especially attractive.

Send for Circular describing hygienic advantages. Terms $2 to $3.50 per day according to location of room and number in room.

HARRISON PHŒBUS, Proprietor.

OLD POINT COMFORT.

Here is built the only fortress which the United States possesses, "FORTRESS MUNROE," so named in honor of President Munroe, and intended for the defense of Hampton Roads, the approaches to Norfolk and the Gosport Navy Yard. Its plan is an irregular hexagon, on two sides of which, comprising the channel fronts, the armament is arranged in two tiers, one in casemate and the other in barbette. It is surrounded by a tidewater moat. The entire Fort covers 80 acres, and cost $2,818,000.

Eighteen miles from Fortress Munroe, on the Elizabeth River, at the confluence of its two branches, are the cities of NORFOLK and PORTSMOUTH and GOSPORT NAVY YARD. A few days may be spent most pleasantly and profitably at these places.

Norfolk is an old but exceedingly pleasant city; noted for the hospitality of its citizens; the abundance and luxury of their tables; fruits and vegetables of all kinds abound; and its fish and oysters surpass all others in the world. From Norfolk, the tourist may visit the *Gosport Navy Yard* by sail or row-boat, and find enough to occupy a day. The *Naval Hospital* is beautifully located on the river, and also *Fort Norfolk*. A drive of ten miles brings you to *Ocean View*, where is a splendid b and views of the Ocean, Capes Henry and Char. Steamers run regularly between Norfolk and Old Point, Cobb's Island, Hampton and other places of interest.

For ocean and water scenery, and the pleasures incident to a seaport town, no place presents greater inducements. The connections of Norfolk are the Seaboard and Roanoke R. R., Norfolk and Petersburg R. R., boats on the James River, the old Dominion side-wheel steamers for New York, and Boston and Providence Line of Steamers from Baltimore, which afford a most delightful coastwise trip.

BALTIMORE & OHIO R. ROAD,
THE OLD RELIABLE DOUBLE-TRACK ROUTE!
WITH

Its Unrivaled Equipment!
Magnificent Iron Bridges!
Unsurpassed Construction!
Gorgeous Mountain Scenery!
New and Superb Hotels!
Fast Time! Air Brakes!
THROUGH CARS!

And all Modern Appliances which conduce to render traveling
SWIFT, SURE AND COMFORTABLE,
Commends itself to the Public as
THE POPULAR ROUTE.

DEER PARK HOTEL,
226 Miles from Baltimore.

OAKLAND HOTEL,
232 Miles from Baltimore.

THROUGH TRAINS

Leave Baltimore at 7.10 A. M. 8.00 A. M. 6 P. M. 8.15 P. M.
and Washington at 8.35 A.M. 7.15 P. M. and 9.25 P. M.

☞ *FOR BERKELEY SPRINGS*
Take same trains as designated above, stopping off at SIR JOHN'S RUN, and staging two miles.

☞ *FOR BEDFORD SPRINGS*
Take same trains as designated above, stopping off at CUMBERLAND.

OFFICES:

NEW YORK, 315 Broadway, and depots foot of Desbrosses and Cortlandt sts.
PHILADELPHIA, 700 and 838 Chestnut street, and depot Broad street.
BALTIMORE, 149 Baltimore st., (cor. Calvert) and at Camden Station.
WASHINGTON, 613 15th st., 485 Penn'a Av. and depot N. Jersey Av. and C. st.
GEORGETOWN, D. C. Masonic Temple, High street, near Bridge street.

THE BALTIMORE & OHIO R. R. ROUTE,

From the Sea to the Virginia Springs, the Mineral Regions of the South, the Great Lakes, and Mountain Ranges of the West.

Charles Carroll, of Carrollton, the the last surviving signer of the Declaration of Independence, laid the corner stone of the Baltimore and Ohio Railroad, July 4th, 1828.

It was designed by its far-seeing originators, to secure to Baltimore the trade and travel of the rapidly growing West. Its great objective point was the Ohio River; to reach which it passes thro' a country of diversified and marvelous beauty and grandeur. This begins at the old RELAY STATION, where the VIADUCT HOTEL is located, at the foot of the Valley of the Patapsco, and where the celebrated THOMAS VIADUCT BRIDGE crosses it: one of the earliest and most complete triumphs of engineering skill in the history of railroads. Its massive stone piers are arranged on a curve, so as to constitute the whole bridge a lateral arch, to make it stronger in resistance to the pressure of the floods and ice of the river. The hotel itself is a handsome and commodious structure, with beautiful surroundings, commanding fine views of the country.

The main stem of the road winds up the valley, following chiefly the course of the Patapsco, whose precipitous banks, mills, villages and waterfalls, entertain the traveler with their beauty and variety.

ELLICOTT CITY, OR MILLS, situated on lofty hills, is a large manufacturing town, possessing many beautiful sites, and is a healthy place for residence or sojourn.

The road from this point continues to ascend, running

POINT OF ROCKS—POTOMAC RIVER.

through many interesting towns and villages. We can only mention a few prominent places on the route.

FREDERICK CITY, 3 miles from Frederick Junction, is nestled in the midst of the Blue Ridge Mountains. The long lofty ridge that trends northeast and southwest, is the Catoctin Mountains. The range beyond is *South Mountain*. Here spreads before us a valley of unsurpassed beauty,—the scene of the Battle of Antietam, enclosing the little town of Sharpsburg.

The city contains about 10,000 inhabitants, has a fine City Hall, Court House, a number of handsome churches and public institutions, and is a place of much refinement and culture. The accommodations for summer recreations are great, and resources for pleasure and health unsurpassed.

The next point of interest is POINT OF ROCKS, on the Potomac River. This is the junction of the Metropolitan Branch of the Baltimore and Ohio Railroad with the Main Stem. All the express trains from the West leave the Main Stem here, and run to Baltimore *via* Washington,—giving travelers an opportunity of visiting the National Capital without extra expense.

The scenery is very attractive. The river cuts through mountains, leaving high cliffs on either side. To the left, in the distance, is *Sugar Loaf*, a point of contention between the Federal and Confederate armies, because it was the best height for observation. At this point Gen. Lee crossed the Potomac when he invaded Maryland and Pennsylvania.

HARPER'S FERRY, in some respects, stands alone among the celebrated places of this country. It is situated at the junction of the Potomac and Shenandoah Rivers, where the two valleys come together ; and there is presented a grandeur and variety of scenery unknown elsewhere.

JEFFERSON'S ROCK—HARPER'S FERRY.

The town is located at the base of Bolivar Heights, the summit of which commands a view actually overwhelming; every locality of which is imbued with tragic incidents of the late war. Three States meet at this point—Bolivar Heights being in West Virginia, Loudon Heights in Virginia, and Maryland Heights in Maryland. Of the view from these heights, Thomas Jefferson said: "It is worth a voyage across the Atlantic to see it."

JEFFERSON'S ROCK, in the vicinity, has a special interest as being the place to which the great statesman after whom it is named used to retire from the vexations of political life, for rest and contemplation. The rock is about 600 feet above the river, supported by four columns of masonry where the natural foundations have been worn away. It is covered with the autographs and inscriptions of visitors. The view from it is one of rare beauty. Directly below it flow the two majestic rivers; near by is Harper's Ferry, with the overshadowing mountains; the grand bridge of the railroad crossing the Potomac; distinctly visible are Charlestown and Sandy Hook, and to the south the Valley of Virginia opens up its incomparable beauty.

MARTINSBURG, twenty miles west of Harper's Ferry, the county-seat of Berkeley, is a renowned old place for health and pleasure; situated on a high plateau west of the Blue Ridge.

Here are the shops of the Baltimore and Ohio Railroad, the scene of the railroad riots in 1877. Several sanguinary battles were fought near this town during the late war. It was the home of Belle Boyd, the heroine.

Near Hancock, on the opposite bank, are the ruins of OLD FORT FREDERICK, built by Gov. Sharp in 1756, for defence against the Indians. It proved to be very serviceable in the war with England, as well as against the savages, but is a shapeless ruin now.

BERKELEY SPRINGS HOTEL, BATH, MORGAN CO., W. VA.

RUINS OF OLD FORT FREDERICK.

Scaling NORTH MOUNTAIN, getting entrancing views of the valley eastward, we arrive at SIR JOHN'S RUN, where James Ramsay, a protege of Washington, launched his steamboat in 1784.* This is the railroad station for BERKELEY SPRINGS, the famous old summer resort of Marylanders and Virginians. The Springs, 2½ miles from the R. R., flow from the sides of the Warm Springs Ridge, 1,200 gallons of water per minute, principally used for bathing, the temperature being 74°. The hotel accommodations are for 700 or 800 guests.

Berkeley Springs were on the extensive estate of Thomas Lord Fairfax, who granted them, with the exception of one known as "Lord Fairfax's Spring," to the Province of Virginia. In 1775, Gen. Braddock's defeated army passed here.

The town of *Bath* was laid out by the Province in 1776, and Gens. Washington, Gates, and other patriots

---

*Twenty-three years before Fulton launched the Claremont at New York.

and colonial gentry, had cottages here, where they spent the summer in hunting and bathing.

CLIFF VIEW NEAR CUMBERLAND.

CUMBERLAND, one of the largest and most important places on the railroad, until 1845 was its western terminus, where passengers westward took stages for Brownsville, on the Monongahela River. It is situated on an elevated plateau, completely surrounded by lofty mountain ranges,—Wills, Nobley's and Dan's Mountains. The scenery here is grand beyond description, and possesses a variety not often viewed even in a mountainous country. Westward reposes one of the loveliest valleys the eye ever beheld, extending thirty miles, through which flows the Potomac River, enhancing its beauty with its silvery waters.

OLD NATIONAL BRIDGE NEAR CUMBERLAND.

The railroad company has recently erected a commodious hotel at this place, specially for the accommodation of summer guests.

CITY OF CUMBERLAND.

For many years, Cumberland was a fortified town, and the fort which formerly stood on the site of the neat little Gothic church in the heart of the city, was the rendezvous for Braddock's expedition. No place in Western Maryland possesses more attractions and matters of historical interest, where the combined resources of health and pleasure are greater. The company has very wisely located here the largest of their hotels, and their wisdom is approved by the immense number of guests who resort hither during the summer months.

This station is the junction of the Pittsburg, Washington and Baltimore branch of the B. & O. R. R., which runs through one of the most interesting and romantic sections of Pennsylvania.

PIEDMONT.—At this place the heavy grade of the road begins, (117 feet to the mile,) requiring two engines to the train. Here we get into the heights of sublimity. The scenery is absolutely grand. On the right is the great SAVAGE range of mountains, at the base of which is the Savage River.

ALTAMONT, 17 miles west, 3,000 feet above the sea-level, marks the region known as the "Glades." This glade region is the summit of the Alleghany country. Near this place the Potomac and Youghiogheny Rivers run in opposite directions,—the Potomac running east and the Youghiogheny running west. The head waters of the Potomac are found near Altamont, not far from Fairfax Stone, the boundary between Virginia and Maryland. In Alleghany County we first find the great coal deposits. Dan's Mountain is the boundary between the two great geological systems. East of it are the limestone and sandstone; west, the great coal measures. The immense Coal Basin lies mainly between Dan's and Savage Mountains; in this valley runs George's Creek, by which this coal region is known.

MOUNT SAVAGE IRON WORKS.

There are mines on every available place for working. So numerous are they, that the whole distance from Mt. Savage to Piedmont (24 miles) is a continuous street of houses, occupied by miners and operatives.

A short distance from this, on Laurel Mountain, Gen. Braddock received his mortal wound, and here his remains repose, in the shade of a venerable oak.

FROSTBURG is in the centre of this mining region; over 2,300 feet above Baltimore. The ascent from Cumberland is very steep, and grades heavy. The mountain under the town is perfectly honeycombed, all the coal having been taken out. The Cumberland and Pennsylvania Railroad passes under it through a tunnel.

From the summit of Savage Mountain, two miles from this town, and 1000 feet above it, the grandest view of the whole route is obtained, stretching over the mountains of Pennsylvania, Maryland and Virginia.

Returning to the track of the "B. & O." the next two stations are DEER PARK AND OAKLAND, and near these, in the most lovely portion of the "Glades," the railroad company has erected two more of their excellent hotels, which are filled with guests during the summer season.

Next we come into the grand CHEAT RIVER country, the most magnificent of all through which this railroad passes; winding westward along the mountain-side, crossing from one dizzy ledge to another on strong bridges or graceful viaducts, while the mountains seem to rise higher and gather their heads closer together in the clouds. The ascent is exciting, 'tis grand; no one as he gazes upon such scenes as "Buckhorn Wall," with its vaulting side and leaping cascade, can but be filled with emotions of sublimity, and reverence to Him whose hand hath set these mountains fast and crowned them with majesty. This may be considered the finest view on the railroad.

The best view of the Cheat River is from the tres-

VIEW OF CHEAT RIVER VALLEY FROM BUCK HORN WALL, B. & O. R. R.

tling of the two bridges over the Cheat and Tray; there we look down into the awful deeps and gaze upward at the sublime heights. Beholding the infinite variety of scenery, of hillside, of valley, of rushing cataracts, of deep gorge and silvery streams, we would wish to stay, admire and adore. But we are hurried on, and from all this magnificence suddenly transferred into the deep darkness of *Kingwood Tunnel*, from which we emerge into another glorious scene; passing through the celebrated coal-gas region we arrive at GRAFTON, the junction of the Parkersburg Branch, where is another of the company's splendid hotels. Here the nearest route branches off to Cincinnati, Louisville and the West.

CLARKSBURG AND PETROLEUM are in the midst of the gas-coal and oil region, of much interest to the tourist as well as to the merchant or manufacturer. At KANAWHA the road strikes the Kanawha River, whose course it follows till it reaches PARKERSBURG, where it crosses the Ohio River over a magnificent iron bridge, which, with its approaches, is $2\frac{1}{2}$ miles long and cost over $1,250,000.

In sight, down the Ohio River, is *Blennerhasset's Island*, where Aaron Burr plotted his treason.

Returning to *Grafton*, we pursue the route to WHEELING, the old "Main Stem" of the road.

Descending through the quiet Tygart's Valley, swiftly passing dense forests, frowning cliffs and leaping cascades, we come to the junction of the Monongahela and Tygart's Rivers, where the united streams are crossed by an iron bridge 600 feet long.

FAIRMOUNT is a neat town, where a suspension bridge crosses the river.

At ROSEBY'S ROCK there is an inscription, stating that on Christmas day, 1852, the finishing rails of the road were laid.

TRAY RUN VIADUCT, CHEAT RIVER.

CHARLESTON, W. VA.

TYGART'S VALLEY AND BRIDGE.

At MOUNDSVILLE we reach the Ohio River. This town derives its name from a great mound, 70 feet high and 1,000 feet in circumference,—one of those ancient and mysterious relics that are found all through the West, the work of a race of whom we have not the slightest historical knowledge. It contains two sepulchral rooms, constructed of logs and stone. Many large skeletons have been found in it; also shell-beads, ornaments of mica and stone, and copper bracelets.

A small rock, with an inscription consisting of 3 lines and 22 characters, was also discovered.

From Moundsville to the city of WHEELING the road runs along the banks of the Ohio River.

WHEELING is a city of considerable importance,—having many large manufactories, especially of *nails*, and is known as the *Nail City*. It was founded in 1769, and has a population of more than 30,000. The road connects here with Washington, Penna., and five miles below, at

Benwood, it crosses the Ohio on a strong, costly iron bridge, to Bel-Air, where it connects by the Central Ohio R. R. with all points West.

THE VALLEY BRANCH ROUTE,
From Harper's Ferry to Winchester, Staunton, the Valley and Springs of Virginia.

Starting from Harper's Ferry, we take the Valley Branch of the B. & O. R. R. to Staunton, Va., a distance of 125 miles.

The Cumberland Valley north of the Potomac, at Harper's Ferry becomes the Valley of Virginia.

In its scenery, historical associations, and battle-fields of the late war, it possesses more interest than any other section of the country. Every mile is attractive, every town has a history or possesses some interesting associations closely connected with the history of Virginia and the United States.

CHARLESTOWN is a fine town, beautifully situated, characteristic of the hospitality and culture of Virginia's best society. It is the place of the trial and execution of old John Brown, from which, if the song be true, his soul commenced its celebrated march.

WINCHESTER, one of the oldest and most noted towns of Northern Virginia. Here the beauty and chivalry of the Old Dominion most frequently met. It retains much of the old Virginia hospitality, culture and customs, and is a favorite place of resort.

It was the most hotly and frequently-contested town in the South during the war, and was the principal entrepot for the lower valley. There is a fort standing here, built by Washington in 1756.

From WINCHESTER stages run to *Capon Springs*, 23 miles, and *Rock Enon*, 8 miles distant.

From *Charlestown* to *Staunton*, the valley is girded

MINERS AT A ROCK-CUTTING.

by vast mountain ranges, with that peculiar blue hue which has given them the name of Blue Ridge. The spacious valley (with its waving fields of grain, its planttations, its villages,) reposes in quiet beauty, guarded by these towering sentinels, whose massive heads rest in the sunshine against the sides of day.

CEDAR CREEK is a romantic place, 46 miles.

STRASBURG, the terminus of the Manassas R. R., the scene of battle and many heroic actions. Here the Massanautton Mountain rears its lofty brow in sublime grandeur over the plains.

WOODSTOCK, EDINBURG and MT. JACKSON, all battle-fields, are beautifully situated: between the last two a *gap* on the east leads into the lovely Luray Valley. Mt. Jackson is the station for Orkney and Shenandoah Alum Springs.

HARRISONBURG, a favorite and somewhat fashionable place, is the station for *Rawley Springs*, 11 miles distant.

The next station, "Weyer's Cave," is 2 miles from the celebrated cave of that name. This cave is the most wonderful and beautiful on this continent, surpassing the Mammoth Cave of Kentucky. A verbal description cannot convey an adequate conception of its strange formation and beauty. In its sublimity and grotesque shapes it is said to excel the Grotto of Antiparos. Its most famous feature is the Hall of Statuary. It has hundreds of other chambers, filled with stalagmites, stalactites and crystals. Far as the light of the torches reach, it reveals marvels of nature's beautiful formations.

STAUNTON, the terminus of the road, is one of the choicest towns in Virginia, renowned in the civil and social history of the valley. It is beautifully situated on a branch of the Shenandoah River, 120 miles from Richmond. It was incorporated 1749, and has ever since borne a prominent part in the history of the country.

CROSSING THE ALLEGHANIES IN THE OLDEN TIME.

THE ROUTES TO WASHINGTON,
The Great Falls of the Potomac, Mount Vernon, the Mountains of Virginia, &c., &c.

The Washington Branch of the B. & O. R. R. was until a few years ago the only line leading to the Capital from the North. It leaves the Main Stem at Relay House or the Viaduct Hotel, crosses the Thomas Viaduct, giving a fine view up the valley of the Patapsco, and in one

hour's run, of forty miles, brings us into Washington, at the foot of Capitol Hill.

Several thrifty towns and villages have sprung up along this road. Among the attractive features of the route, we may enumerate Irving Park, an inviting forest for Excursionists—the cultivated fields and groves of the Maryland Agricultural College—the old Calvert Mansion, once the favorite resort of Henry Clay—the battle-field and duelling ground at Bladensburg—and as we approach Washington, a cluster of palatial villas at every hand.

THE BALTIMORE AND POTOMAC RAIL ROAD passes under Baltimore through a splendidly constructed tunnel; thence skirting its western boundary, crossing Gwynn's Falls on a high bridge in the rear of the House of Refuge, passing Loudon Park Cemetery with its grand old forest trees; gaining another extended view of the city and bay;—"dodging under arches, flying over bridges,"—crossing the eastern branch of the

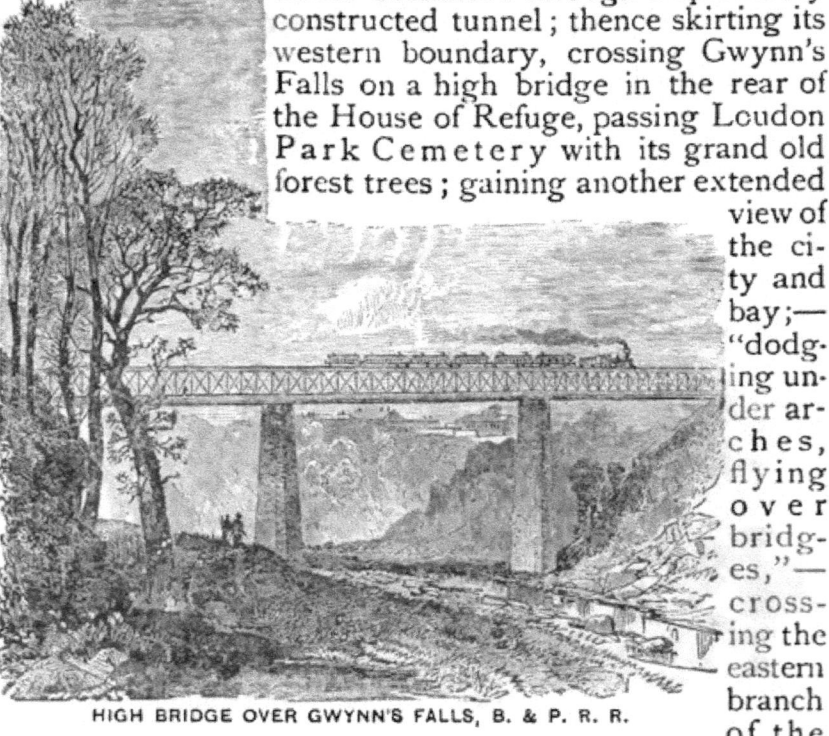
HIGH BRIDGE OVER GWYNN'S FALLS, B. & P. R. R.

Potomac just as we had gained a glimpse of the Capitol, and plunging into another tunnel, emerges at the Washington Navy Yard; entering the metropolis at the elegant and commodious Sixth-street depot.

In order to get the most comprehensive view of the city and its surroundings, let us ascend to the dome of the Capitol and take a general observation.

From the upper gallery of the dome, exalted 300 feet above the Potomac, we get a view of great beauty. In the distance the hills of Maryland roll to the North and

East. Westward lie the heights of Virginia, chief of which is Arlington, crowned with Arlington House, renowned as the palatial residence of John Parke Custis, where the marriage ceremonies of Gen. Washington took place in January, 1759. The property descended to Geo. Washington Parke Custis and his daughter, who married Gen. R. E. Lee in 1832. During the late war the United States Government took possession of it, and dedicated the grounds around the mansion for a national cemetery, where 15,000 soldiers are buried. The Potomac River flows majestically down between those heights and Washington.

Gazing over the city itself, you will notice that the broad avenues radiate from Capitol Hill, stretching away to its remotest limits,—designed, perhaps, to express the national sentiment of unity, bearing, as they do, the names of the States of the Union.

Directly beneath us, between Maryland and Pennsylvania avenues, are the magnificent National Conservatories and Botanical Gardens, filled with the choicest native and exotic plants and trees. To the left, beyond these, is the *Mall*, above the trees of which arise the quaint towers and walls of the SMITHSONIAN INSTITUTE; an effort to revive the mixed architecture of the middle ages, and producing about as inconvenient and ill-appointed a building as could be devised. Beyond this looms up the roof of the building of the DEPARTMENT OF AGRICULTURE, the grounds of which are perhaps the most beautiful in Washington. Just below these stands the unsightly, unfinished shaft of the Washington Monument; a monument to the shame of the American people,—a mournful testimony of their unfulfilled pledges to the memory of their great deliverer and Pater Patriæ.

Northwest of this, and near the river, we perceive the two domes of the National Naval Observatory, in which there is the largest equatorial telescope in the world, which has already made some valuable discoveries.

Carrying your view further to the west, you discover a city spreading over the heights and nestling among abundant forest trees. It is the old city of Georgetown; the heights are called Georgetown Heights. Back of the town is the Reservoir, which supplies the two cities with water from the Potomac; and OAK HILL CEMETERY, the gift of W. W. Corcoran, the most refined and lovely resting-place for the dead in this country.

To the right of this the eye rests upon the magnificent forests of the "Soldiers' Home," a park for natural beauty not to be surpassed anywhere. This is maintained as a home for invalid and aged soldiers who have served their country faithfully in war. It affords the most beautiful drives in the vicinity of the city.

Looking up Pennsylvania avenue, we perceive the Treasury Building, with its long colonnade; beyond it the President's House and the new State Department. Across the avenue is the CORCORAN ART GALLERY, the munificent gift of Mr. Corcoran, whose wealth and taste have made it one of the most interesting and valuable art galleries in the world. In some respects it is decidedly superior to any other. The collection consists of statuary, paintings, bronzes, casts, and many objects of *virtu*. The building is a costly one and unusually well adapted to its purpose. The nation cannot be too grateful to Mr. Corcoran for this beautiful and costly consideration for its education in art.

The CAPITOL we shall not attempt to describe. It is a grand edifice. While not perfect in its architectural proportions or beauty, yet one of the greatest buildings of modern times, and worthy at least of a day's study and examination. It contains many works of art which are amply described in the special guide-books.

The visitor who has but a short time to survey Washington, should begin at the Capitol, this being by far the most important, and thoroughly explore and appreciate it before undertaking anything else. Thence he should visit the Botanical Gardens, Smithonian Institute and Agricultural Bureau, the Treasury, President's House, State Department, the Arsenal and Navy Yard. Having seen these public and national places, if he has time he should visit the other institutions, especially the *Louise Home*, built by Mr. Corcoran, as a refined home for elderly ladies who have become reduced from affluence to want; named for his wife whom he lost early in life, whose memory he has thus beautifully consecrated by a most noble and unique charity.

The other buildings which the tourist will visit are the Post-Office and Patent Office, standing opposite each other on F street, between Seventh, Eighth and Ninth; the Masonic Temple, opposite on Ninth; the Old Capitol Building, used as a prison during the war, &c. There are hundreds of other places of interest in and near the city which we have not the space to mention.

Washington is fast becoming one of the most beautiful and interesting cities in the world, and increasing in importance not only as a political but a scientific centre.

The tourist will not fail to make the usual trip down the Potomac to Mt. Vernon, and pay his patriotic respects to the home and tomb of Washington, and at the altar where *his* pure patriotism was kindled, revive his own devotion to his country. The trip is a pleasant and instructive one. On the way you pass Forts Washington and Foote; the ancient and historic city of Alexandria, where Washington it may be said commenced his public career, and where he has left many enduring evidences of his patriotism.

Mt. Vernon belongs to the people of the United States.

By contribution they purchased it, and they have full control over it, through a board of patriotic Lady Regents, one from each of the States and Territories. It is eighteen miles below Washington, and occupies one of the most beautiful and romantic sites to be found on the banks of the Potomac. Its great attraction is, however, to be found in the fact that it was the home of Washington, that there he lived and died, and there he and his wife quietly repose. Mt. Vernon has therefore become the Mecca to which Americans annually make pilgrimages. Among the objects of interest to be found in the old mansion are pictures of the Washington family, the key of the Bastile presented to Washington by Lafayette, and others. The lid of Washington's white marble sarcophagus is wrought with the arms of his country, and has simply inscribed upon it the one name, "Washington."

THE VIRGINIA MIDLAND ROUTE.

To the Virginia Springs, the Historic Scenes of the Late War, and the Great South.

The Virginia Midland Road, extending from Alexandria to Danville, Va., forms a great Trunk line to all parts of the South in which the tourist may find pleasure and comfort.

Leaving Washington from the beautiful depot of the Baltimore & Potomac R. R., we cross the Potomac River on „the long bridge," from which we get fine views of Washington, Georgetown Heights, Arlington, etc., and in a few minutes arrive at Alexandria. This is a quaint old city, wearing very much the aspect it wore in revolutionary days, when it was the residence of the Virginia aristocracy. Its streets still bear the names given them in colonial times: as Kings, Queens, Princess, York, Fairfax, &c.

It contains a number of buildings associated with revolutionary and colonial times, among which is Christ Church, (built in 1773 with bricks brought from England.) In this church Gen. Washington worshipped, and his name is borne on the roll of its first vestry; his pew remaining precisely as it was when he occupied it. Washington Lodge is also a place of great interest. Members of this lodge take pleasure in pointing out to visitors the chair used by Washington when he presided as its master, and which has been used by every master of the lodge since his day. Washington Free School is also a monument of the munificence of the Pater Patriæ—it is situated on Washington street and still fulfils its mission.

The old Braddock Mansion, now a part of the Mansion House Hotel, is also a relic of the past worth visiting, especially as it is in excellent order and always accessible. It was the home and headquarters of Gen. Braddock when he planned the disastrous campaign in which he lost his life, in 1754. This superb old mansion was built in 1732, of stone. The house in which Col. Ellsworth was killed by Capt. Jackson is now occupied as a store, but is still pointed out as an interesting relic.

Probably no city in the Union has more revolutionary reminiscences than this good old town. It was emphatically the city of Washington, and was intimately connected with his every-day life. La Fayette had also his headquarters here, at the southwest corner of King and Pitt streets, and the building still remains very much as it was in his day. But this whole section of country is historic ground.

MANASSAS STATION is on a portion of the memorable battle-field of Bull Run. The road here connects via STRASBURG, with the B. & O. R. R., for the north and

THE UNIVERSITY OF VIRGINIA—FOUNDED BY JEFFERSON IN 1819.

west; while to the south, CULPEPPER, RAPIDAN, CEDAR MOUNTAIN and many other names recall the mournful memories of the late war.

GORDONSVILLE is a noted station in the midst of a beautiful country. It was a great commissary depot of the Confederates. The road here connects with the Chesapeake & Ohio R. R., for Richmond and the Ohio River.

CHARLOTTESVILLE is the seat of the University of Virginia, where centers much of the educated and refined element of Virginia society. Near by, situated high up on the mountain-side is MONTICELLO, the home of Thomas Jefferson. Here the road connects with the Chesapeake and Ohio, for the White Sulphur and other Springs.

LYNCHBURG, a characteristic Virginia town, spreading over hills and valleys, is one of the healthiest of places. It is in the near vicinity of the great Blue Ridge Mountain ranges, and consequently is a fine place for the tourist and invalid to spend a portion of their time. Here the R. R. connection is with the Atlantic, Mississippi & Ohio R. R. for NORFOLK, PETERSBURG, BRISTOL, KNOXVILLE, CHATTANOOGA and the great Southwest, running through the most magnificent portions of the United States from the Mississippi River to the Atlantic Ocean.

DANVILLE, the terminus of the Virginia Midland R. R., is on the State line between Virginia and North Carolina. The road here connects with the air-line for Texas and the Gulf States.

The longest line of Pullman cars in the world runs by this route from Washington to New Orleans. The company have arranged a number of routes by their road and its connections, which greatly facilitate travel from distant points, securing comfort in accommodations, and unbroken connections,—forming a great through route, via the Capitol of the United States, from the North to the South, Southwest, and the famous Virginia Springs.

VIRGINIA MILITARY INSTITUTE, LEXINGTON.

THE SPRINGS AND NATURAL CURIOSITIES OF VIRGINIA.

The Virginia Springs, to some of which allusion is already made, are found in the highlands of Virginia and West Virginia, mostly amid the high ranges of the Alleghany and Blue Ridge Mountains.

The scenery in the midst of which they are situated is perfectly grand: it is sublime. Hills roll above hills, gathering height until they reach their climax of grandeur in the skies rivers rush adown their sides, and through deep gorges, bathing the feet of these titanic monarchs; cascades chase each other from dizzy heights to the valleys; mists clothe the mountain brows, while the sun gilds their awful sides and crowns them with diadems of glory.

Those of easy access by the railroads leading from Baltimore, are the Augusta Springs in Augusta Co. (alum and chalybeate;) Bath Alum, in Bath Co.; Capon, in Hampshire Co., W. Va.; Rock Enon and Jordan's Rock Alum, in Frederick Co.; Rawley, in Rockingham Co., said to be the best pure chalybeate in the State; Rockbridge Alum, in Rockbridge Co.; Sweet Springs, in Monroe Co.; Yellow Sulphur, in Montgomery Co.; Greenbrier White Sulphur, in Greenbrier Co. These are among the best known; not only for the medicinal qualities of their waters but as the favorite resorts of the gay, fashionable and genial people of the South.

THE NATURAL CURIOSITIES OF VIRGINIA are also grouped in this remarkable section of country. WEYER'S CAVE, with its vast galleries peopled with Nature's exquisite statuary; MADISON'S CAVE, with its no less exquisite draperies; the BLOWING CAVE; the NATURAL BRIDGE, with its vast single arch, the wonder and admiration of every beholder; the sublime PEAKS OF OTTER, rising abruptly more than 4,000 feet above the plain, and 5,307 above the level of the sea; MARSHALL'S PILLAR, an immense column of rock 1,000 feet in height; the wonderful ICE MOUNTAIN, with its strange stores of the pure crystal; CAUDY'S CASTLE and the beautiful natural fountain of the TEA TABLE, with its generous laver—clothed with exquisite ferns and velvet mosses—forever overflowing with its sparkling tide.

The Hawk's Nest, or Marshall's Pillar, is on New River, in the county of Fayette, a few rods from the main turnpike leading from Guyandotte to the White Sulphur Springs—ninety-six miles from the former and sixty-four from the latter place. It consists of an immense column or pillar of rock, rising perpendicularly to the height of 1,000 feet above the river. It is called Marshall's Pillar in honor of the late venerable Chief Justice, who, as one of the State Commissioners appointed to reconnoitre that section of country for the

VIEW FROM THE HAWK'S-NEST OR MARSHALL'S PILLAR.

location of a public improvement, stood upon its dizzy height and sounded its exact depth to the margin of the river. Our illustration gives the view from the top of the pillar, looking west, but does not convey an adequate idea of the height of the pillar itself.

A foreign traveler thus beautifully describes the elevating and sublime emotions with which he was inspired on visiting it:

"You leave the road by a little by-path, and, after pursuing it for a short distance, the whole scene suddenly breaks upon you. But how shall we describe it? The great charm of the whole is connected with the point of sight, which is the finest imaginable. You come suddenly to a spot which is called the Hawk's Nest. It projects on the scene, and is so small as to give standing to only some half-dozen persons. It has on its head an old picturesque pine; and it breaks away at your feet abruptly and in perpendicular lines, to a depth of more than one thousand feet. On this standing—which, by its elevated and detached character, affects you like the monument—the forests rise above and around you. Beneath and before you is spread a lovely valley. A peaceful river glides down it, reflecting, like a mirror, all the lights of heaven, washes the foot of the rocks on which you are standing, and then winds away into another valley at your right. The trees of the wood, in all their variety, stand out on the verdant bottoms, with their heads in the sun, and casting their shadows at your feet, but so diminished as to look more like the pictures of the things than the things themselves. The green hills rise on either hand and all around, and give completeness and beauty to the scene; and beyond these appears the gray outline of the more distant mountains, bestowing grandeur to what was supremely beautiful."

EAGLE CLIFF AND FALL, HAVANA GLEN.

THE NORTHERN CENTRAL ROUTE,

To Gettysburg, Harrisburg, Watkins Glen, Havana Glen,
the Falls of Niagara, the Lakes and the
Garden Counties of New York.

NO SECTION of the country presents a greater variety of beautiful Scenery than that through which the NORTHERN CENTRAL RAILWAY passes. From its starting point in Baltimore to its terminus, every mile is pleasing. Taking the beautiful little valley of Jones' Falls, it affords picturesque views of the most highly cultivated and adorned suburban country of Baltimore. Cutting through the high rolling hills of Maryland, it brings us into the great farm lands of Pennsylvania, an agricultural country not surpassed if equalled. Along the water-courses are factories and iron furnaces, whose busy spindles by day and fiery flames by night, give unceasing interest to the journey.

The places of resort and recreation to which this road leads are abundant.

MT. WASHINGTON, a suburban village, presents many attractive features to render it a desirable place of residence.

LAKE ROLAND, 9 miles from Baltimore, is a charmingly romantic place. The Lake has been beautifully improved and utilized as a water supply for the city. It reposes in a lovely valley, surrounded by green, rolling hills, many of which are crowned with pretty suburban villas. It is three or four miles in extent, and winds in graceful curves along its banks, displaying new attractions at every turn. The shores are in the very highest state

"BRIGHTSIDE," LAKE ROLAND.

of cultivation—lawns carefully cropped, and trees, shrubs and flowering plants arranged and cultivated for park effect. In the dreamy summer evenings, when dotted over with gaily decorated boats, and enlivened with music, and the echoes of joyous voices, the scene is one of rare attractiveness, and is widely appreciated as among the most delightful of our Summer Resorts. The charming villa of "BRIGHTSIDE" and others in the vicinity, are largely patronized.

LUTHERVILLE, (11 miles from Baltimore,) is the most attractive village on the line of the Northern Central Railway. Here is located a Lutheran Seminary of learning. The country adjacent is undulating, and the beautifully-improved grounds of the residents give it the appearance of a "garden of flowers." Seven trains northward and six trains southward stop at this station daily, except Sunday.

GLENCOE, (20 miles,) is becoming a place for families to spend the hot, dusty months of summer, where there are beautiful drives and shady walks. The proximity to the city, and accommodating trains, make it a convenient place for business men to spend the summer with their families.

Through this diversified and highly cultivated region, there are many other places of summer retreat, such as PARKTON, NEW FREEDOM and YORK.

HARRISBURG, PA., the northern terminus of the Baltimore Division of the N. C. Railway, the capital of the State, is beautifully situated on the Susquehanna River. It is a city well worth visiting.

Four magnificent bridges span the river, (which is about a mile in width,) so constructed as to resist the pressure of the floods and ice, making the crossing perfectly safe. Four railroads centre here: the Cumberland Valley, Pennsylvania, Northern Central and Philadelphia and Reading. There are many objects and places of interest, viz: the Public Buildings, State and Municipal; the State Library, containimg 40,000 volumes; the monument erected to the memory of the soldiers who fell in the Mexican war; and a splendid opera house.

Northward of Harrisburg the scenery becomes more grand and presents views that are peculiar to this region. Passing through the centre of Pennsylvania, into the western portion of New York, the traveler is entranced with a succession of views, frowning precipices, mountain torrents, dashing, foaming cataracts, awful chasms, shady glens, pastoral fields, sublime scenery of every variety.

We particularize the matchless views along the canal near *Millport: Watkins' Glen*, renowned for its wild, wierd scenery, its wonderful chasms and cascades, as the

SENECA LAKE, N. Y.
278 miles from Baltimore,
132 miles from Niagara,
278 miles from New York.

"Cathedral," "Artist's Dream;" *Havana Glen*, with its "Bridal Veil," "Mystic Cascade" and "Eagle Cliff and Fall."

SENECA LAKE.—This is one of the most charming and romantic of lakes, and reminds one of Lake Geneva in Switzerland. It is 40 miles long and from two to five in width. Its water is clear and cool, with a dark green shade, and it is a remarkable phenomenon that it *never freezes over*.

The Senecas, from whom the lake derived its name, was one of the six Indian nations that dwelt among the hills of New York.

There are some interesting legends connected with the lake, especially that of Agayentah, the great and noble chief of the Senecas, who was struck by a lightning bolt which threw his body down the mountain-side into its waters. When the storm rages and the thunder rolls, the lake guns are heard, and Agayentah's spirit is on the war-path. The guns are the echoes of his voice marshaling his forces in battle. The lake guns will be heard so long as there is an Indian on this continent.

WATKINS' GLEN is at the head of this lake, and the lovely town of Geneva, called the "gate to the garden counties of New York," is at the foot. It is celebrated for its schools and colleges and its great nurseries covering over 800 acres.

NIAGARA FALLS is only five hours ride from Geneva —the grandest of all attractions for the tourist—which no pen can describe and no pencil adequately depict.

ENTRANCE TO CATHEDRAL, WATKINS GLEN.

GRAND SUMMER RESORT

AND TOURISTS' HOME.

GLEN PARK HOTEL,

THE LARGEST HOTEL IN WATKINS,

And Nearest the Entrance to

THE FAMOUS WATKINS GLEN.

THIS SPACIOUS AND POPULAR HOTEL has recently been thoroughly repaired and re-fitted, and the present management guarantee that its accommodations shall be first-class and excelled by none. It is situated on the main avenue and most convenient to all places of interest.

With its broad piazzas, its half-flight stairways, airy and well ventilated rooms, *en suite* or single, and lighted by gas, beautiful and highly ornamented grounds and shady walks, superior springs of pure water from the hillside for culinary purposes, and its mineral springs for drinking and bathing, and its excellent *cuisine*, render the **GLEN PARK** the *ne plus ultra* for all seeking quiet rest and relief from cares, or for amusement and profit, by a sojourn in this region of glens and romantic scenery.   C. S. FROST, PROPRIETOR.

☞ Terms, $2 $2.50 & $3 per day.   Free 'bus to trains & boats.   Hacks 25c

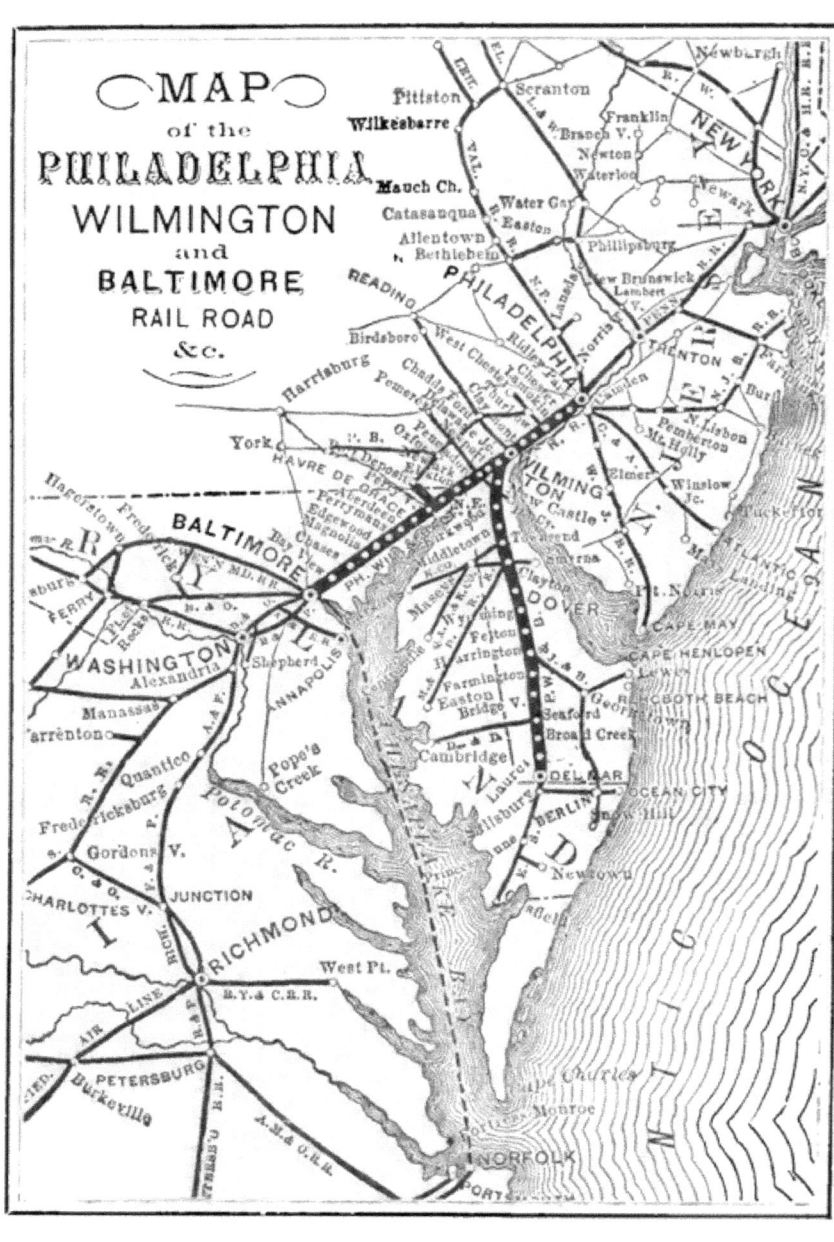

THE PENINSULA ROUTE,

Via the Philadelphia, Wilmington and **Baltimore R. R.**, to the **Garden Lands** of Maryland and Delaware, and the **Sea-Bathing Resorts of the** Peninsula.

This Route, extending from Baltimore to Philadelphia, is the connecting link between the North and South,—crossing Maryland and Delaware.

Its views are peculiar, consisting of wide river and bay scenes.

Going North, the tourist first has a fine view of Baltimore Harbor: Locust Point, with its immense elevators and European steamers; Canton and its great factories, rolling-mills and packing-houses; Fort McHenry in the distance, and the headwaters of the bay.

Over the Gunpowder and Bush Rivers, which widen at their mouths to a mile, the railroad crosses on low pile bridges.

Recently the company have transformed the humble station HAREWOOD into a beautiful resort and excursion grounds, at a considerable expense,—fitting it up in attractive style, and supplying it with abundant resources for pleasure parties.

HAVRE-DE-GRACE, (a small, quaint town, on the Susquehanna River,) is 40 miles from Baltimore. The peculiar feature of this place is the magnificent *Truss Bridge* over the river, one mile in length. The view from the bridge is beautiful; looking up stream, we are presented with a charming vista; the river flows down between high bluffs, and is divided by a picturesque island. Below the bridge, the river expands into the proportions of a bay. HAVRE-DE-GRACE is a place of historical interest, associated with the brave exploits of Count Pulaski and General Lafayette, in 1777, and suffered from invasion by the

British forces under Admiral Cockburn in the war of 1812.

On the north bank, six miles above, the noted little city of PORT DEPOSIT nestles under the hills.

ELKTON, the next station of interest, is on the Elk River, where Sir William Howe landed with his army in 1777, and marched thence to Philadelphia. Admiral Cockburn threatened an attack upon it in 1813. It marks the boundary between the North and South—Mason and Dixon's Line.

WILMINGTON, DEL., is the largest and most important place on the road, comprising about 40,000 inhabitants. It is situated on the Delaware and Brandywine Rivers, and was settled by the Swedes. It contains a number of buildings, relics of the ancient Swedish style, chief of which is "the old Swedes' Church," near the railroad depot, now owned by the Episcopalians. The first Dutch landing was made in 1616. Wilmington is noted for its immense iron ship-building, car and machine shops, the celebrated Dupont Powder Mills, and other manufacturing industries. This is the head of

THE PENINSULA ROUTE.

By this route we reach the "Garden Spot" of Maryland. So the Eastern Shore has ever been regarded by its denizens,—a claim not disputed by those who have visited it and enjoyed their hospitality.

The peninsula is 180 miles long, and 70 broad at its widest part,—embracing the entire State of Delaware, nine counties of Maryland and two of Virginia. The area included is about 6,000 square miles.

The EASTERN SHORE AND DELAWARE RAILROAD extends from Wilmington to Crisfield on the Chesapeake Bay. Five roads branch from it to various points, on or near the bay and Atlantic Ocean, viz: Queen Ann and Kent R. R., to Centreville; Kent Co. R. R. to Chestertown (from Middletown); Maryland and Delaware R. R. to Oxford; Dorchester and Del. R. R., to Cambridge;—Junction Road, to Lewes and Rehoboth; and Wicomico and Pocomoke R. R., to Berlin and Ocean City.

The introduction of these roads has produced a revolution in this section, and evoked a spirit of enterprise which is raising the public estimation of it as an agricultural and commercial locality. Under the hand of modern progress, the "old times" are fast passing away.

The first place of interest below Wilmington is NEW CASTLE, cosily reposing on the banks of the Delaware. Until recently it seemed to belong to the last century, lazily pursuing the paths its fathers trod, under the old land grant of William Penn, the income of which paid the municipal expenses. Under the inspiration, however, of the Tasker Iron Works, it has awakened to a new life, and manifests decided improvement. Steamers are now taken from this point to CAPE MAY—the greatest sea-bathing resort on the Atlantic coast.

KIRKWOOD, the next town of importance, is the centre of a rich country. Here the great peach district begins. MOUNT PLEASANT and MIDDLETOWN are two great peach stations; the latter, especially during the season, presenting a lively appearance. Our illustration gives a fine representation of the scenes that daily occur at the station. Stages run from Middletown to WARWICK and CECILTON, MD., and ODESSA, DEL., where Commodore McDonough, one of our naval heroes of 1812, was born.

TOWNSEND, the next station, 4 miles below, is the junction of the road to Centreville.

At CLAYTON, 37 miles from Wilmington, there are two branch roads,—one leading east, to Smyrna, a beautiful town; the other to the west, running southwest 54 miles through Caroline and Talbot counties to EASTON,

MIDDLETOWN, IN THE HEIGHT OF THE SEASON.

described by Bayard Taylor as "a high, clean, cheerful place, still keeping its old-time mansions, but keeping them in good condition." OXFORD, eleven miles from it, is the terminus on the bay, of the Maryland and Delaware R. R. Returning to the main road, we run down to the flourishing town of DOVER, the capital of the State of Delaware. It contains 2,000 inhabitants. It is $47\frac{1}{2}$ miles from Wilmington, in the midst of a highly-cultivated country. A large canning and fruit-packing house here has given an impetus to industry.

WYOMING, 50 miles from Wilmington; CAMDEN, WOODSIDE, FELTON, HARRINGTON, are all interesting places.

MILFORD is the most important town in Delaware, south of Wilmington. It is a large manufacturing place; has many handsome residences, churches, and a live newspaper, ably edited, through whose influence the place has greatly improved.

LEWES, the terminus of the Junction and Broadwater Road, at Cape Henlopen, opposite Cape May, is an old town, founded in 1683, and is a favorite summer resort. Six miles below is REHOBOTH CITY, where are the great camp-meeting grounds of the M. E. Church.

Returning to SEAFORD, we there take the Dorchester and Delaware R. R. for CAMBRIDGE, the terminus on the bay, one of the noted towns "embowered in luxurious shade, with ancient houses, built of bricks brought from England, and with gardens neat and trim."

DELMAR, the last large town on the Delaware Road, is the junction with the Eastern Shore Railroad. Six miles below which is SALISBURY, the chief business place of the peninsula, near the Trappe district, the birth-place of Samuel Chase, a signer of the Declaration of Independence, one of Maryland's most distinguished patriots, appointed to the supreme bench by Washington. From

WATER CRAFT AT CRISFIELD.

Salisbury, via the Wicomico and Pocomoke R. R., we reach BERLIN, and six miles further on the Atlantic Ocean—Coffin's Beach,—where the sea bathing is unsurpassed if equaled on the coast.

PRINCESS ANNE is a fine old town of 1,000 inhabitants, with an ancient colonial Episcopal church built 1670.

NEWTON, at the terminus of the Worcester and Somerset R. R., is an enterprising place, significant of the new era dawning upon Eastern Shore.

WESTOVER is in the centre of a cluster of splendid estates, which illustrate the former history of the old proprietary families. Since the war these have changed hands and begin to assume a modern aspect.

KINGSTON has become quite a place of resort for Northern people. Near by is the mansion of Hon. S. R. Dennis, U. S. Senator from Maryland.

CRISFIELD, one hundred and thirty-five miles from Wilmington, is situated on Tangier Sound. It is the great oyster port, being surrounded by the finest and most bountiful oyster-beds in the bay.

We advise tourists to take a trip down the peninsula without fear of being disappointed. It bristles at every point with features of attraction—beautiful inlets where the angler or the sportsman may find exciting pastime, or extended shores where the breakers invite to their embrace the adventurous bathers ; for the sea-bathing resorts of the peninsula cover its whole stretch of coast from the Delaware to the Chesapeake.

Bayard Taylor, describing his tour through it, observes: "We do not travel many miles before the characteristics of the peninsula scenery begin to exhibit themselves ; its prevailing English character, (old farm-houses of stone or brick, spacious gardens and orchards, frequent hedges, smooth rich fields, and the lush, billowy green of deciduous woods,) is still retained."

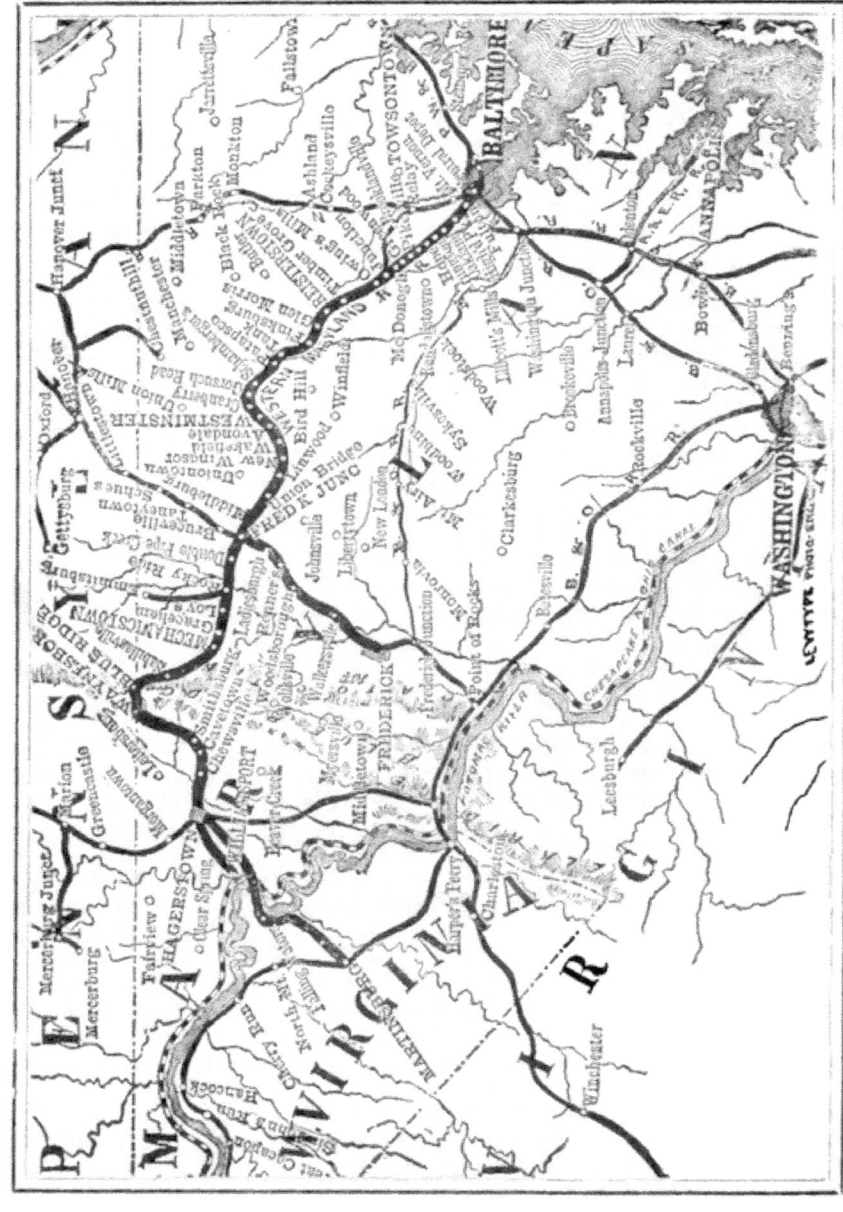

THE WESTERN MARYLAND RAILROAD ROUTE.

The United States present a greater variety of scenery than any country in the world; and the multitude of railroads, runing in every direction, bring this marvelous variety rapidly into view,—changing from plain to mountain, from seaboard to inland scenery, from the cultured field to wild forests, from broad rivers to narrow gorges and leaping cascades. The observing traveller or tourist finds in the ever-changing panorama a ceaseless source of entertainment.

The Western Maryland Railroad illustrates this very finely. Emerging from the tunnel of the Baltimore and Potomac road at Fulton Station, on the western limits of the city, our view extends over an expanse of country, of rolling hills and vales. To the east, the city, with its compact streets, its spires and monuments, presents a pleasing contrast to the rural scenes on the west. This portion of the suburbs of Baltimore is unsurpassed for diversity of scenery and high state of cultivation.

From Fulton Station the road soon crosses the beautiful valley of Gwynn's Falls, to the right of which rise the hills of DRUID HILL PARK. We get glancing views of its grand old trees and its adjoining palatial homes, as we are whirled along.

HIGHLAND PARK is next passed to the left, the graceful tower of its magnificent hotel rising above the grand old forest trees, peering through which we gain occasional glimpses of the beautiful villas by which it is surrounded. We now pass a number of stations situated in the midst of a beautiful open country, peculiarly adapted for

PAVILION AT GREENWOOD PARK.

HIGHLAND PARK HOTEL.

the homes of business men of the city. ARLINGTON is peculiarly attractive in this respect; so is MOUNT HOPE, the seat of the celebrated Asylum for the Insane; and PIKESVILLE, one of the old neighboring localities of Baltimore which the railroad has introduced into a new era.

GREENWOOD, an important station, where the company has laid out a large, handsome park, with an elegant pavilion and inviting lakes in sight of the road; a quiet, cool and safe retreat from the noise and heat of the city, and supplied with every facility for the use of excursion parties.

MCDONOGH—deriving its name from the McDonogh Farm and Manual Labor School, endowed in the will of the late John McDonogh—is an interesting spot to visit.

OWINGS' MILLS, an old town, renowned as the station for the rich butter and cream which supplies in part the tables of Baltimore. The surrounding country, for dairy products, is not excelled.

OWINGS' CREEK.

SCENE IN GREENWOOD PARK.

EMORY GROVE, nineteen miles from Baltimore, at the head of Worthington Valley, is the Station for the Emory Grove Camp of the Methodist Episcopal Church; an attractive spot, admirably chosen for the purpose.

WESTMINSTER, an attractive city, the county-seat of Carroll, situated at the headwaters of Patapsco, on Parr's Ridge, 33 miles from Baltimore, and 1,000 feet above tidewater. It was founded in 1766 by an English family, who named it Winchester, afterwards changed by an Act of Assembly to Westminster. Its surroundings are very fine. From College Hill we have a magnificent view, extending from the Potomac to the Susquehanna Rivers. The buildings of interest are the Western Mary-

OWING'S CREEK SCENERY.

land Female College, under the patronage of the Methodist Episcopal Church; the Court House, and several handsome churches. It has a number of banks, a savings institution, a gaslight company, two ably-edited weeklies, two hotels and a large manufacturing company. Its population is about 3,000, comprising some of the most cultured people in the State. It is therefore, socially, as well as otherwise, a delightful place of resort.

Seven miles beyond is NEW WINDSOR, adorning an elevated plateau, in the celebrated Pipe Creek region, where farming has reached its highest state. The New Windsor College is located here, in full view from the cars. Iron and copper ores abound in the vicinity, and some of the finest quarries of marble in the State.

LINWOOD, UNION BRIDGE and MIDDLEBURG are in the Pipe Creek country. Little Pipe and Big Pipe Creeks are branches of the Patapsco River, which afford fine water-power and fertilize a large scope of country.

UNION BRIDGE, originally called "Buttertown," was made a post village in 1810, and received its present name. To this town belongs the honor of having given birth to the reaping machine. Jacob B. Thomas, a resident, in 1811 made the first machine, with an automatic attachment, which he set to work in his fields. It was partially successful, but the ridicule of his neighbors deterred him from further efforts; and his cousin, Obed Hussey, taking his machine for his model, reaped the glory of its invention himself. This was also the home of Maryland's great sculptor, Rhinehart, and it was in a quarry near by that he first gave form and life to marble.

YORK ROAD is at the junction of the Frederick division of the Pennsylvania Railroad, five miles from which, on that road, is the noted little place TANEYTOWN, a place of pleasant resort. Below, at the terminus, seventeen miles distant, is—

HIGH BRIDGE ABOVE MECHANICSTOWN.

Frederick City, beautifully situated in a fertile valley, in many respects the most interesting inland city of Maryland. (See page 15.) It enjoys the reputation of being one of the healthiest and most charming of our resorts, has fine hotel accommodations, an abundant water supply direct from the mountains, live newspapers, and a social and hospitable community. One of Baltimore's most enterprising citizens, Mr. Louis McMurray, has located an immense packing establishment near the city, the Mountain Sugar-Corn Factory, the largest in the world, having a capacity of 75,000 cans a day. He has a farm of 1,200 acres under thorough cultivation, capable of producing a million and a half cans of corn annually. The Maryland Institution for the Instruction of the Deaf and Dumb is also beautifully located here, having a capacity for three or four hundred pupils.

Rocky Ridge is the station where passengers change cars for Emmittsburg, (seven miles distant,) in the centre of a splendid mountainous region. To the west, "Jack's Mountain" and "Carrick's Knob" are seen rising in majestic height, sloping gracefully into the beautiful valley. The scenery here is strikingly grand and the air pure.— Emmittsburg contains a number of interesting public institutions, St. Joseph's Academy, Mount St. Mary's College, and others.

We now start on the ascending grade toward the Blue Ridge, and emotions of sublimity are aroused at every step of our progress ; above Mechanicstown, where we begin to scale South Mountain, we cross a high bridge, which affords us splendid views in every direction; at Sabillasville, in the Harbaugh Valley, there is a piece of engineering skill, in the Horse-Shoe Curve, which gives us an encircling sight of the mountains and valley. The ascent is exciting ; gradually it unfolds more of the panorama below us, until passing Blue Ridge Summit,

CUMBERLAND VALLEY, FROM WAYNESBORO' STATION.

VIEW FROM CROWN CLIFF.

1500 feet above tide water, well known as a resort for excursionists, and near which are numerous mountain hotels and Springs, we arrive at WAYNESBORO STATION, where suddenly bursts on our view a scene of surpassing beauty; it is the Cumberland Valley — indescribable — once seen never to be forgotten. Virginia, Maryland and Pennsylvania, unite in spreading out their beauty over this incomparable valley. In order to afford visitors a better opportunity of viewing this scene in all its grandeur, the Railroad Company has graded a fine carriage drive from Waynesboro Station to CROWN CLIFF, a point less than two miles distant, where buildings have been erected for the entertainment of excursionists, and where from the Pavilion perched on the summit of the cliff, the view is indescribably sublime. In the distance the hotel

GERMANTOWN GORGE, BLUE RIDGE.

at Monterey Springs is clearly discernable; and fields, farms, dwellings and spires enliven the landscape, and the substantial Switzer barns lend their characteristic feature to the picture for miles away. It was on this lofty summit that Mason and Dixon and their party, when running the line between the possessions of William Penn and Lord Baltimore, tarried awhile to enjoy the chase in the midst of this magnificent scenery, then draped in its primeval grandeur. Near by also is "Harman's Gap," through which Allan Cameron and the Tory refugees from Canada penetrated under the guide of the Indian chief "White Eyes," the ally of the British, in order to join the Hessians under Knyphausen and the British tories under Gen. Gage and Lord Dunmore, to destroy the town of Frederick.

Throughout the descent of the western slope, the wonderful panorama of the Cumberland Valley is spread before the passenger, seated at the car window.

HAGERSTOWN, the county-seat of Washington County, is a thriving, important city. The Western Maryland Railroad, the Cumberland Valley and the Baltimore and Ohio Railroad centre here, affording ample facilities for travellers and tourists from all sections. It is situated in a rich, lovely valley, surrounded by some of the most highly-cultivated farms in the State. The population is about 7,000, governed by a mayor and city council; the press ranks high among the journals of the State, and the bar and pulpit are filled with men of a high order.

WILLIAMSPORT, the terminus of the road, is situated on the Potomac River at one of its most interesting points, 90 miles from Baltimore, at its junction with the Conococheague, and the Chesapeake and Ohio Canal.

Here we have splendid views of the Potomac River and valley, the distant mountains of Virginia, enhanced in interest by many of the most startling occurrences of

POTOMAC RIVER AND CANAL AT WILLIAMSPORT.

the late war. The Confederates crossed the Conococheague at this place through the canal aqueduct, by turning out the water. Williamsport is a large depot for coal transported by canal boats.

The five hours trip over this road reveals all the peculiar features of Central and Western Maryland; productive farms, with their plain homesteads, huge red barns, plentiful orchards, turnpike towns of distinctive Dutch aspect, wide spreading meadows, lofty rock-ribbed hills, mountain masses, smoking furnaces; features so different from those of eastern and southern Maryland, as to make it seem like another clime.

DEEP CUT ABOVE MECHANICSTOWN.

GREENBRIAR WHITE SULPHUR SPRINGS.

THE CHESAPEAKE BAY.

Its Summer Retreats and Sea-Bathing Resorts.

The CHESAPEAKE BAY is unsurpassed by any inland sea in the world for the advantages it offers for invalids and pleasure-seekers. The Mediterranean Sea is interesting mainly for its classic shores, cities and towns identified with ancient and mediæval history; but the Chesapeake Bay, with its wide expanse of water, balmy yet bracing air, its many quiet towns and watering-places, its facilities for excursions, is without a rival.

It is remarkable for its extreme irregularity of coast-line—numerous bays, estuaries on either side, serving as outlets to the different waters of Maryland and Virginia. The region drained by the bay and the waters flowing into it embrace an area of 70,000 square miles.

Numbers of steamers ply between Baltimore and the numerous places of interest on its Eastern and Western Shores. During the summer season, in addition to regular trips, steamers make excursions to various bathing and pleasure resorts, the most interesting of which are CAMBRIDGE, the county-seat of Dorchester county, beautifully situated on the Choptank River, 18 miles from its mouth, and on Cambridge Creek,—having a water front on two sides. The river is two miles wide, presenting a beautiful view, and affording fine bathing, sailing and fishing.

It is a town of great antiquity, as shown by the style of its buildings. It contains 3,000 inhabitants, and many persons of refinement and culture. It is the terminus of the Dorchester and Delaware R. R., connecting with the Peninsula R. R. at Seaford.

EASTON, the county-seat of Talbot county, is located near the navigable waters of three rivers: Tred-Avon, Miles River and the Choptank. It was incorporated in 1874. It is one of the most fashionable places on Eastern

Shore, a centre of wealth, gaiety and culture. On account of its associations, no less than its situation, it is a delightful place to visit. It has about 3,500 inhabitants. It is on the Maryland and Delaware R. R., which terminates ten miles below, at OXFORD, a beautiful little town of 500 inhabitants, on Third Haven River near the mouth, looking out to the bay. The scene here is quite charming: a number of beautiful islands dot the bay and mouth of the river; and on the various points of land and surrounding shores are some of the finest farms in Maryland. It contains two fine hotels, situated at the water's edge, with bathing shores.

ST. MICHAELS, twelve miles from Easton, on St. Michael's River, is one of Easton Shore's most attractive and sprightly towns. Its streets are lighted at night and sidewalks nicely paved. It has nearly 2,000 inhabitants.

DENTON, the county-seat of Caroline county, on the great Choptank River, is remarkably pleasant. Its main street presents a beautiful appearance, being shaded by rows of maple and Georgia poplar trees. The public buildings stand on a beautiful square, filled with shade trees,—making it a pleasant resort for the citizens. During the summer evenings it is enlivened by croquet players.

KENT ISLAND, the largest island in the bay, fifteen miles long, was the site of the first white settlement in Maryland. It lays between Chester River and Eastern Bay, presenting a long front to Chesapeake Bay, and separated from the main land by Kent Narrows. The population is about 1,500.

CHESTERTOWN, the county-seat of Kent, one of the oldest and most fashionable places in Maryland. "Laid off" in 1706; was a port of entry, and erected a number of large warehouses and fine residences. In 1752 it had a handsome town hall and theatre. It is beautifully situated on Chester River, sixty miles from Baltimore. The population 2,000. Near it is the venerable Washington College founded in 1783.

Kent County has furnished many of the distinguished men of Maryland in legal and commercial pursuits.

CRISFIELD, at the extreme point of Somerset, on the Little Annamessex River, four miles from its mouth, looks out upon the bay through Tangier Sound. It is the southern terminus of the Eastern Shore R.R., has regular steam packets and sailing vessels plying between it and Baltimore.

The WESTERN SHORE of the bay contains many places of interest and pleasant resort. Steaming down the Patapsco from Baltimore we pass a number of points, recognized by their Light-Houses, bearing names familiar to pilots: Rock Point, Bodkin Point, Stony Point, Persimmon Point, Sandy Point, Hurdett's Point, Greensbury's Point, the last being at the mouth of Severn River, which we enter and land at ANNAPOLIS, the ancient Capital of Maryland.

ANNAPOLIS was colonized by Puritan refugees from Virginia, and chartered in 1708. Being centrally located, it became the social and political capital of the State. Although it waned as Baltimore grew in commercial importance, it never lost its "court character," and has always been the focus of legislative, judicial and intellectual power.

The gentry of the old and new world made it the place of their residence and erected mansions of brick, imported from England, which stand to-day the quaint, pleasing reminiscences of the style and elegance of our luxurious ancestry. The principal objects of interest are the STATE HOUSE and the NAVAL SCHOOL,—the former as decidedly colonial as any building in the land. It is purely English in style and construction, and is an interesting study. From its dome, 200 feet above the waters of the Bay, you have a panoramic view of a wide scope of country.

In front of the door is a fine bronze sitting statue of Chief Justice Taney, by Rinehart. In the House of Delegates is Peale's original full-length portrait of Washington, accompanied by Gen. Lafayette and Col. Tilghman. In the Senate Chamber, Congress met in 1782, and ratified the Treaty of Peace with Great Britain. Here Washington resigned his commission as commander-in-chief of the army, and here the war was really ended, and the independence of the States assured. This Hall has never been changed, but wears the same look as when Washington (represented in a picture now hanging on its wall) stood within it and tendered his resignation. No other building in the United States, now standing, is so consecrated with the memories of our revolutionary history.

THE NAVAL ACADEMY, established by the efforts of George Bancroft, and opened October, 1845, with its beautiful grounds, is well worth, of itself, a day's visit.

Leaving Annapolis Roads, we pass Tally's Point and Thomas Point Light-house, and steam into SOUTH RIVER, nine miles from Annapolis, which drains a large section of Anne Arundel county, and, about three miles further south, WEST RIVER,—both affording many shipping points for the farmers and truck gardeners. Hundreds of crafts ply these rivers, bringing to market the famous Anne Arundel fruits and vegetables. The lands along these rivers are the chief grain-producing farms in the county. Ten miles down the coast we come to FAIR HAVEN in Herring Bay, one of the most delightful summer resorts on the Chesapeake, sixty miles from Baltimore. It has a fine hotel and pleasure-grounds looking out upon the bay. The Weems line of steamers make regular daily trips during the season.

From this point to the mouth of Patuxent River, the shore of Calvert county extends, unbroken by bays and river-mouths as above. At the mouth of this river is DRUM POINT, the terminus of the Drum Point R. R.—Packets coast down to Plum Point, Governor's Run, and the Patuxent River; making a delightful run up that river, to Hill's Landing.

The Patuxent River divides the old counties of Calvert and St. Mary's. The latter is the southern county of Maryland, on the Western Shore of the bay—the oldest in the State—terminating at POINT LOOKOUT, at the mouth of the Potomac River, below Acquia Creek, Virginia; both noted places during the late war.— At Point Lookout, a fine monument is reared to the memory of the Confederate prisoners who died there. This place and Piney Point, a few miles above, have become watering-places, celebrated for their invigorating air and good bathing shores. Steamers from Washington make regular landings here.

Further up the Potomac, at Colton's and Blakiston's, good accommodations for summer resort have been provided, and they are visited by many from Washington and Baltimore. We are here on interesting historical grounds. There is a group of islands, named by Lord Baltimore "Herons," from the vast number of those birds found there. The largest of these he called St. Clement's, (now Blakiston,) and was the place where he first set foot with his Colony in Maryland, March 25, 1634. They touched here on their ascent of the river. Father White, one of the Colony, thus writes: "On the day of the annunciation of the blessed Virgin Mary, March 25, we offered the first sacrifice of the Mass,—never before done in this region of the world." Bancroft says: "A cross was planted on this island, and the country was claimed for Christ and England."

They then ascended the river to Piscataqua, opposite Mt. Vernon; but fearing to settle so far inland among the savages, returned to St. Mary's River, about ten miles above Point Lookout. They cast anchor in it four miles above its mouth, at the Indian village, Yoacomico; by treaty took formal possession of it March 27, 1634; named it St. Mary's City, and made it the seat of government, and it continued to be the capital until the ascendancy of the Puritans in 1692, when it was transferred to Annapolis. The great legislative assembly was held in St. Mary's City, February 26, 1635. Scarcely a vestige of the Colony exists, and the site of the capitol is now occupied by St. Mary's Female Seminary.

The trip to Washington by the Potomac River is exceedingly pleasant and interesting, and to the intelligent tourist full of points of historic interest. Besides those already described, the other places of interest are

GLYMONT, a popular resort for Washingtonians, cosily nestled on the Maryland shore, among the hills.

FORT WASHINGTON, whose natural beauties are enhanced by the government grounds and buildings.

MT. VERNON, the home and tomb of Washington, from which one of the most magnificent views of the river is obtained.

ALEXANDRIA, six miles below Washington,—described on pages 31 and 32.

Above GEORGETOWN the river narrows, the banks are more precipitous, and the current more rapid. The scenery undergoes a decided change, becoming more wild and entrancing. At GREAT FALLS the view is grand; the river leaping over the ledges of primitive rocks, forming a splendid cataract, and making a foaming, waving current below. It is so easy of access that pleasure parties from Washington frequently spend the day there, returning at night.

WESTERN MARYLAND RAIL ROAD.

General view of the famous Crown Cliff, 2000 feet above tide water, one of the highest peaks of the Blue Ridge. The grandeur of the scene from this crag cannot be portrayed by tongue or art, and is not surpassed by that from Mt. Washington or the famous "Peaks of Otter." During the late war it alternated as one of the principal signal stations of the Confederate and Federal armies in the great Pennsylvania campaign.

Best Excursion Road in the State.

Numerous Medicinal Springs, Mountain Hotels and Summer Resorts throughout its line.

SCENERY MAGNIFICENT!
SPECIAL INDUCEMENTS TO EXCURSIONISTS!

Greenwood Park, Blue Ridge, Crown Cliff, Cumberland Valley, *AND MANY OTHER POINTS, OFFER THEIR ATTRACTIONS TO TOURISTS OR EXCURSION PARTIES.*

B. H. GRISWOLD,   J. M. HOOD,
    Gen'l Ticket Agent.   *Gen'l Manager.*

CONGRESS HALL, CAPE MAY, N. J.

FOR CAPE MAY.
PHILADELPHIA, WILMINGTON and BALTIMORE R. ROAD TO NEW CASTLE,
AND STEAMER TO CAPE MAY.

Passengers leaving President street Station, Baltimore, at 9.55 A. M. on TUESDAYS, THURSDAYS and SATURDAYS, will connect at New Castle with the commodious and stanch steamer RICHARD STOCKTON

FOR CAPE MAY

Fare—Baltimore to Cape May..$3.50
Fare—Baltimore to Cape May and return 6.00

WILLIAM CRAWFORD, General Agent.

CANFIELD, BRO. & CO.
BALTIMORE, MD.

Watches, Clocks, Diamonds, Jewelry,
SILVER WARE AND SILVER-PLATED WARE,
Tea Sets, Ice Water Sets, Pitchers, Baskets, Casters,
KNIVES, FORKS, SPOONS, &c.
FRENCH CLOCKS,
Bronzes, Fancy Goods, Gold and Silver-headed Canes,
Field and Opera-Glasses, Polished Brass Goods,
Umbrellas, Fans, Spectacles, Eye-Glasses.
MEDALS AND BADGES FOR SCHOOLS AND COLLEGES.
AMERICAN WATCHES A SPECIALTY.

THE BALTIMORE TYPE FOUNDRY,
No. 7 Bank Lane, (Adjoining Barnum's Hotel,)

GEO. B. RICKETTS & CO., (late LUCAS) Proprietors.

PRINTERS' MATERIAL
of every description, always on hand.

We Electrotype in a superior manner, and guarantee our work first class.

FORT WILLIAM HENRY HOTEL,
LAKE GEORGE.

This magnificent house, with its splendid appointments adapted in every particular to the comfort and convenience of families and guests, is now open, at prices to suit the times. Three dollars per day, and *$12, $15, $17.50 and $21 per week*, according to location of rooms.

T. ROESSLE & SON, Proprietors.

Important Arrangement.

Passengers going north or south on the Delaware and Hudson Canal Co's Rail Roads, or through Lake Champlain, can have their baggage checked by way of Lake George on application to Conductors of trains and Captains of steamers, by payment of the usual fare between Baldwin and Glen's Falls.

EXCURSION TICKETS WILL BE GOOD FOR TWO DAYS.

Steamers leave the wharf in front of the house daily for Fort Ticonderoga, Lake Champlain, Montreal, &c. Every convenience for Boating, Fishing, Sporting, etc.

TO HALIFAX, NOVA SCOTIA.

ALLAN LINE, ROYAL MAIL STEAMSHIPS.
Summer Schedule 1878.

S. S. HIBERNIAN, 3,200 tons. Capt. Lt. F. Archer, R. N. R.
S. S. CASPIAN, 3,100 tons.............. Capt. M. Trocks.
S. S. NOVA SCOTIAN, 3,200 tons..... Capt. W. Richardson.

These Iron Screw Steamships are all double engined and are built in water tight compartments; they are unsurpassed for strength, speed and comfort, and fitted up with all the modern improvements that practical experience can suggest for trans-Atlantic service. An experienced Surgeon is attached to each vessel. Cabin passengers are allowed 20 cubic feet of baggage. Passengers arriving at Baltimore to take our steamer for Halifax etc., can have their baggage checked from train to steamer.

RATES OF CABIN PASSAGE.

From Baltimore to Halifax, or vice versa................$20 gold,
Excursion Ticket to Halifax and return.................$35 gold,
From Baltimore to St. John's, N.F., or vice versa,......$35 gold,
Excursion Ticket to St. John's N.F., and return.........$65 gold.
Children between one and twelve years, half fare—under one year *free*.
The above prices include everything except wines, etc.
First class Cabin to Liverpool.........................$75 gold.
For further particulars address A. SCHUMACHER & CO.
General Agents, 5 South Gay street, Baltimore, Md.

☞ This trip commends itself to all who wish to enjoy a delightful and comparatively novel SUMMER RESORT, as well as the advantage of a short ocean voyage by a *first-class trans-Atlantic Steamship*. These vessels are all fitted up in the most luxurious style, being supplied with all the modern appliances for making an ocean voyage both safe and agreeable. The trips between Baltimore and Halifax average 3½ days, 12 to 15 hours, during the day time, on the beautiful Chesapeake Bay, and three days on the Atlantic.

HALIFAX, with its fine harbor, and the exquisite beauty of the surrounding country, possesses all the allurements of a first-class Summer Resort, such as Boating, Fishing, Hunting, Sea-Bathing, etc. and the temperature, agreeable during the day, is delightfully cool at night.

Excellent Hotel accommodations can be had at from $2 to $3 per day, and such visitors as prefer it, can always obtain good board in the suburbs from five to eight dollars per week.

Washington City, Virginia Midland & Great Southern Rail Road

JOHN S. BARBOUR, Receiver,

RUNS FROM WASHINGTON TWICE DAILY

TO ALL THE VIRGINIA & WEST VIRGINIA SUMMER RESORTS,

With close connections from Baltimore and the Eastern Cities.

Evening train has sleeper through to Greenbrier White Sulphur—twenty five miles the shortest route——Best connections to the South and West——Through Sleepers from Washington to Savannah, Washington to N. Orleans and New York to Lynchburg—connecting at Lynchburg for Memphis and all Texas. Call on W. L. BAILEY, 149 Baltimore st. Baltimore, or H. L. PEYTON, 160 Penn'a Av. Washington, D.C.   J. M. BROADUS, *Gen. Ticket Agent.*

IMPERIAL HOTEL,

FIRST CLASS

Pennsylvania Avenue,   WASHINGTON, D. C.

Room and Board, per month.........................$50.00
"   "   "   per week 17.50
"   "   "   per day ....$2, $2.50 & $3.00

To meet the wants of the Traveling Public, this First-class Hotel has reduced its price from $4 to $2, $2.50 and $3 per day

The above Hotel is pleasantly located near Fourteenth St. fronting on Penn'a Avenue, is convenient to the Treasury, Army, Navy, State, Post Office, and Interior Departments.   *JAMES S. PEIRCE, Proprietor.*

THE HAMILTON,

Corner 14th and K Streets, opposite Franklin Square

WASHINGTON, D. C.

A Select Family Hotel, containing all conveniences, including Hale's Elevator. Situated on elevated ground, and open at all seasons, it is especially commended to Tourists and seekers of pleasure, who desire to view the Capital in its summer dress, when its Fountains, its cultivated reservations, its attractive drives and its Suburban Retreats are all to be seen to the best advantage.

ROCK ENON SPRINGS,

ON THE GREAT NORTH MOUNTAIN,

Near Winchester, Va.,

A. S. PRATT,..........Proprietor and Manager.

A Home for the Refined and Intelligent.

Terms, $40 to $50 per month, according to room.

No Bar on or near the premises.

For pamphlets apply to A. S. Pratt & Son, 401 9th st., Washington, D. C.

MORRISETT HOUSE,

ON THE EUROPEAN PLAN

No. 75 MAIN STREET, next to Post Office,

NORFOLK, VA.

BOARD, $2.00 per day.   T. MORRISETT, Proprietor.

HAGADORN BROTHERS,

Hotel Printing

A SPECIALTY!

Hotel & Rail Road Advertising,

No. 5 South Calvert Street,

BALTIMORE, MD.

FORT WM. HENRY HOTEL,
LAKE GEORGE.

This magnificent house, with its splendid appointments adapted in every particular to the comfort and convenience of families and guests, is now open, at prices to suit the times. Three dollars per day, and $12, $15, $17.50 and $21 per week, according to location of rooms.

T. ROESSLE & SON, Proprietors.

STIEFF

HIGHEST AWARD AT THE CENT[ENNIAL]
Diploma of Honor and Medal of M[erit]
FOR
GRAND, UPRIGHT AND S[QUARE]
PIANOS

The principal points of superiority in the Stieff Pianos are h[igh] quality of tone, with great power — evenness of touch thr[ough] entire scale — faultless action — unsurpassed durabili[ty]

UNEXCELLED WORKMAN[SHIP]

A LARGE VARIETY OF
SECOND HAND PIA[NOS]
OF ALL MAKERS,
Constantly in store, and ranging in prices from $75

We are also Sole Agents for the Southern States
Matchless Burdett, Taylor & Farley, and Peloubet
ORGANS.

A full supply of every style constantly in store, and sold on t[erms]. For terms, and Illustrated Catalogues of Pianos [or Organs] Address CHA'S M. STIEFF, 9 N. Liberty st. Baltim[ore]

www.ingramcontent.com/pod-product-compliance
Lightning Source LLC
Chambersburg PA
CBHW020900160426
43192CB00007B/1004